Your competition is with yourself

Shirena Aktar

In loving memory of my grandmother.
Nothing feels complete without you.

Preface

Your competition is with yourself sends a message to children 'you can only be better than what you were before so you compete with your past self and be the best that you can be today'.

Winning games and races is all fun and fulfilling. But not losing heart if you lose is also winning. Be happy for others and understand that we all are different and unique. Everyone has strengths and weaknesses, and nobody is perfect. We are all on different journeys in life.

This book is the first book from a series. Through my books I aim to teach children self-love, appreciation, building empathy towards others, controlling negative emotions and enforcing positive feelings.

I began writing these books when I saw my children have learned how to read and now, they can gain an understanding of what they are reading. So, I wrote them something to read that will be beneficial for them.

Master Mindful books not only give strength to children but also, they are a great reminder for adults who are reading them including myself.

I hope you enjoy my book.

Thank you

Shirena Aktar

Master Mindful is our teacher. He is always very polite. He's kind, he's caring, he is wise, he is daring. He is funny. He is smart. He is creative and loves art. Sometimes he can be annoying though. Especially when he laughs. It is so loud and squeaky! It goes through me.

WHO IS THE
BEST?

He gave us a task today. He does, every day.

Today, our task is to find out who is the best. "Are you the best?" He asked. List your good and bad qualities and let's find out!

Sandy is the best at skipping, she can also tie her shoes, she's good at singing songs, she has great moves, but she never eats all her food.

50+50=100

Muezza is good with numbers. He plays basketball, he's very friendly with others, and he is very tall. When we have a race, Muezza always comes last, even with his long legs.

Adam is very brave, it's like he came out of a cave. He's super at climbing rails and he catches all the snails. He is so full of energy. He is as fast as electricity. However, Adam can be very moody when he does not get his own way.

I'm
tired

Luke is our helpful hero; he never scores zero. Excellent writing, excellent spelling. Excellent drawing and excellent snoring. He loves to sleep. When we all want to play, he wants to sleep. He's always tired.

Laura is wealthy, she's got the latest gear. She's also very healthy and has no fear. She knows all about history and can solve mysteries, but Laura struggles with maths. She hates that class.

hmmmmmm???

So, Master Mindful asked, now we know everyone's strengths and weaknesses. Can we decide who is the best?

"Hmmmmm.... we can't," said the children.

Master Mindful told us we are all unique and different and we must not compare ourselves with anybody. Nobody is perfect or better than anyone else.

Your competition is with yourself.

Everyone is Unique
Aim Higher
One Player
Happy for others
Well Done

Let's always try and be the best
that we can be, said Master Mindful,
as we are all truly amazing.

Acknowledgements

First of all, I would like to thank my children, it is because of them that the idea came to mind. I started reading my work to them. 'Ten out of ten,' my eldest son said. Seeing his excitement made me excited and eager to publish my material to the world.

I am forever grateful to my parents who have always been there for me in good times and bad. I appreciate everything you have done for me and could not thank you enough.

My sister and my auntie have always supported me in every challenge I have faced. Without you both, starting this journey would have been impossible. Thank you for believing in me and encouraging me to pursue my dream.

I would also like to thank my husband and the rest of my lovely family and great friends who gave me confidence and strength.

Thank you to Isaac, who has beautifully illustrated my book, and Daniel Mc Cain, who is my project manager.

Thank you all.

About the Author

Shirena Aktar

Born and brought up in England, United Kingdom. Shirena is self-employed and works as a freelance counselling tutor. Shirena also helps out in a women's wellbeing group to fight loneliness and depression.

Shirena believes counselling is helping people help themselves. Problems and situations cannot always be changed, but the way we view it and react to it most certainly can.

Shirena Aktar is a married woman and a mother of four young children. Whilst reading books and making up stories at bedtime for her children, Shirena aspired to writing powerful stories which encourage good behaviour and lift self-confidence.

Shirena Aktar is a new author who has written a series of children's fiction books of which the first one has now been published for you and your children to enjoy and benefit from.

Master Mindful Books

1. Your competition is with yourself

2. Change with change

3. Think before you act and better you will react

4. All in good time

5. Let's be considerate and kind

6. Never give up

7. Communication is the key, solve your problems and be happy

8. Say bye bye to bad feelings

9. Make the most out of every moment

10. A reminder to myself